DIY Dreams Catcher Crochet For Adults

Make Your Room More Fascinating!

Copyright © 2020

DEDICATION

Contents

Crochet Basic Dreamcatcher

Dreamcatchers are said to act as dream filters, allowing only good dreams to reach the sleeper! We have put together an easy crochet dreamcatcher and we want you to put it to test! You can use an embroidery hoop and any color yarn (I use white in my example). The more colors you use, the more colorful it gets.

You can pair this dreamcatcher with as many decorative items you or your little ones can dream of. Happy dreams!

What you need

Embroidery hoop 10 cm diameter

Worsted weight yarn (I used white)

4.00 mm & 4.5 mm (G/6 & 7 hook)

Tapestry needle

White thread

Decorative items (beads, fabric scraps, ribbon, lace, cords, yarn)

Instructions

Hoop

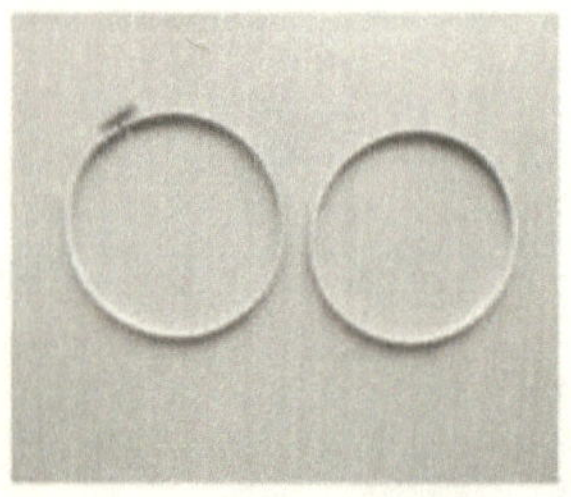 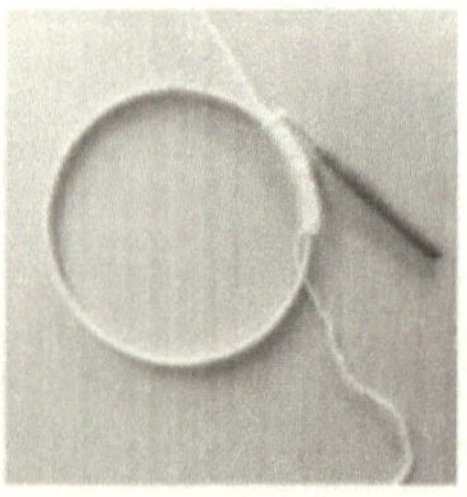 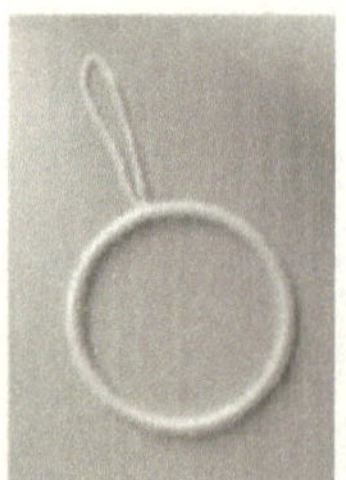

First take aside your hoop; we will be needing only the inner hoop. Using white yarn and 4.5mm (US. 7) hook, sc around the hoop, ss, to the first sc, to join. Ch 60 and ss, to joining st, to create the hanger. Fasten off.

Doily

Using white and 4.00 mm hook (US G/6) Start with a magic ring or ch 4 and ss, to first ch to form a ring. Rnd 1: Ch 3 (counts as first dc), 11 dc into magic loop/ or ch 4 ring. Slip into 3rd chain of beginning ch 3. (12 sts).

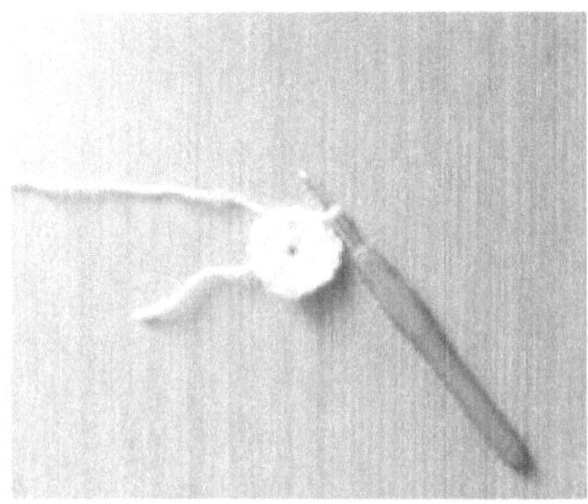

Rnd 2: Ch 5 (counts as dc, ch 2). (Dc, ch 2) in each stitch around. Slip into 3rd chain of beginning ch 5. (12 dc and 12 loops)

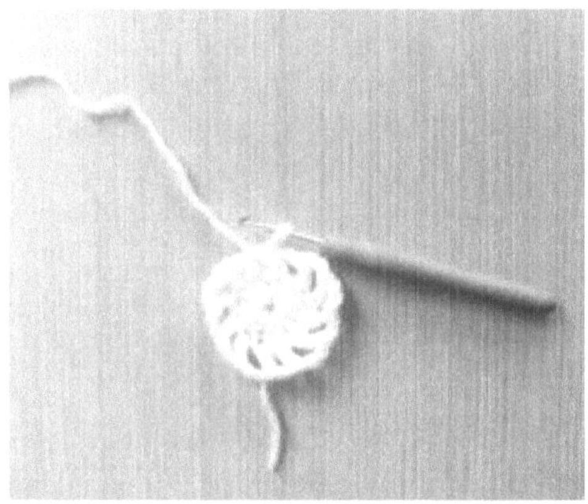

Rnd 3: Slip into ch 2 space. *(Dc, ch 2) twice into ch 2 space. Dc, ch 2 in next ch 2 space. Repeat from * around. Slip into first dc. Bind off. (18 dc and 18 loops)

Rnd 4: Sl st in ch-1 sp, ch 1, sc in same sp, ch 6, [sc in next ch-1 sp, ch 6] around; join with sl st to first sc. (18 sc and 18 ch-6 sps)

Rnd 5: Sl st in ch-1 sp, ch 1, sc in same sp, ch 7, [sc in next ch-1 sp, ch 7] around; join with sl st to first sc. (18 sc and 18 ch-6 sps)

Fasten off.

If your hoop is smaller just work fewer Rounds. If it is larger repeat Round 5, but increase the number of working chains in each Round. For example Round 6 would be: [sc in next ch-1 sp, ch 8] around.

Assembly:

Using your tapestry needle sew the doily on the hoop. Alternatively use some white thread and tie the edges of the doily to the hoop with thread.

 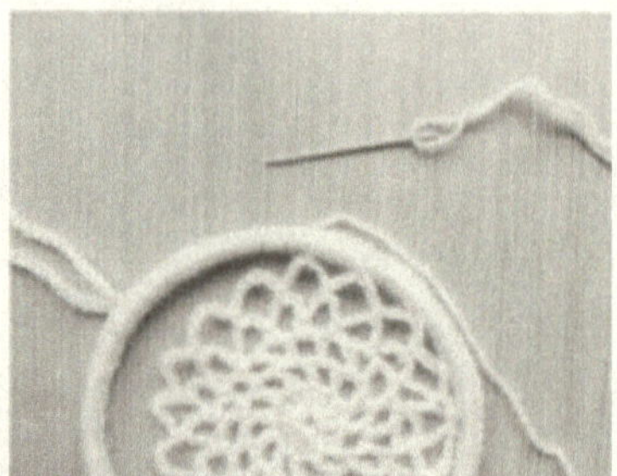

Make up:

Gather all your decorative items, lace ribbon etc. and start tying to the bottom of your dreamcatcher. Using yarn make a long chain and tie to the bottom of your dreamcatcher. If desired add beads, or feathers.

 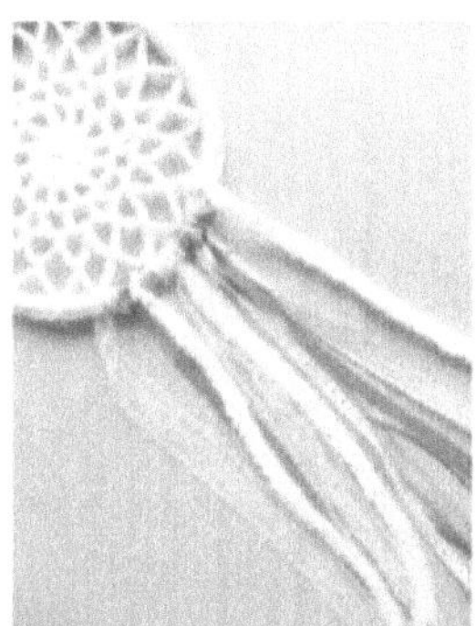

That's it! Enjoy your dreamcatcher!

Crochet Feather Dreamcatcher Pattern

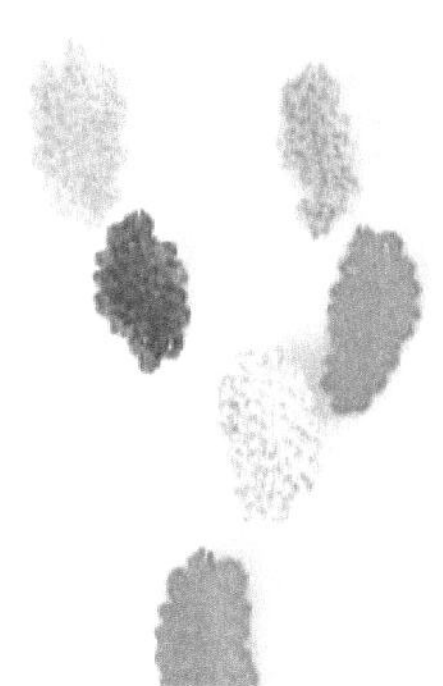

What you need

Materials:

Crochet thread – white

Crochet yarn – 5-6 bright colours

Crochet hook – 1.5 mm and 3 mm

Scissors

Craft wire – 22 gauge

This project include the following stitches (US terms) – single crochet (sc); slip stitch (sl st) and chain (ch). For the doily pattern you may need double crochet (dc) stitch.

Instructions

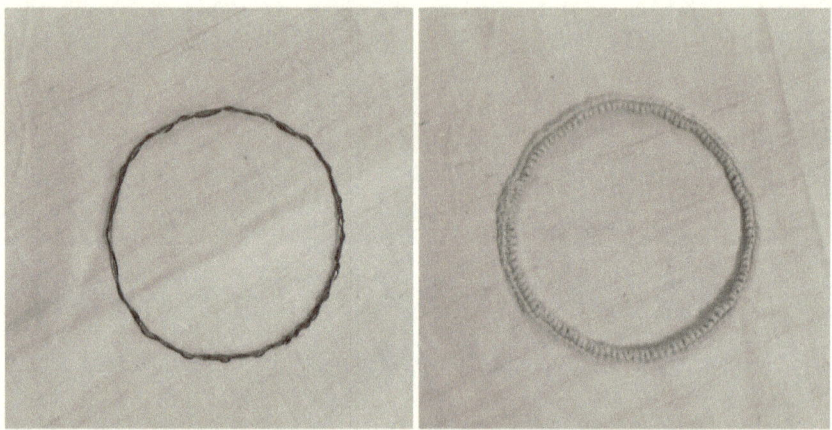

Use a 22 gauge craft wire to form a base ring for the dreamcatcher. Use a light coloured or white yarn to cover the ring. I did sc around the ring to cover it.

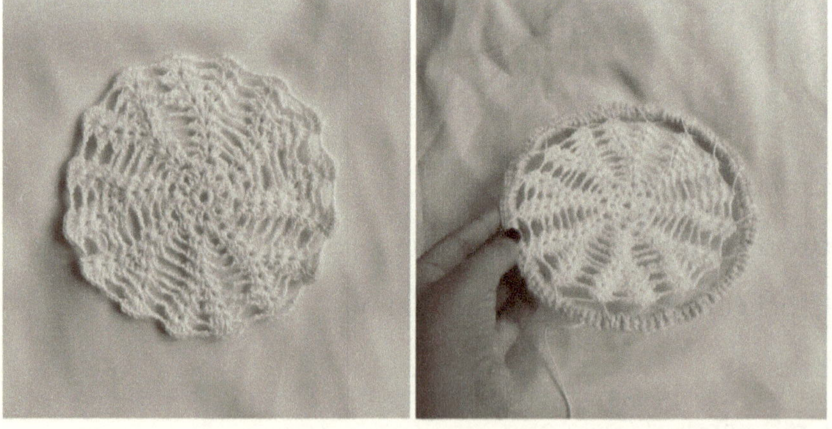

The doily: Use white crochet thread to create the doily, use any pattern you want. The size of the doily would also depend on your choice or required size of the dream catcher.

Place the doily on inside the ring and stitch the doily with the ring all around.

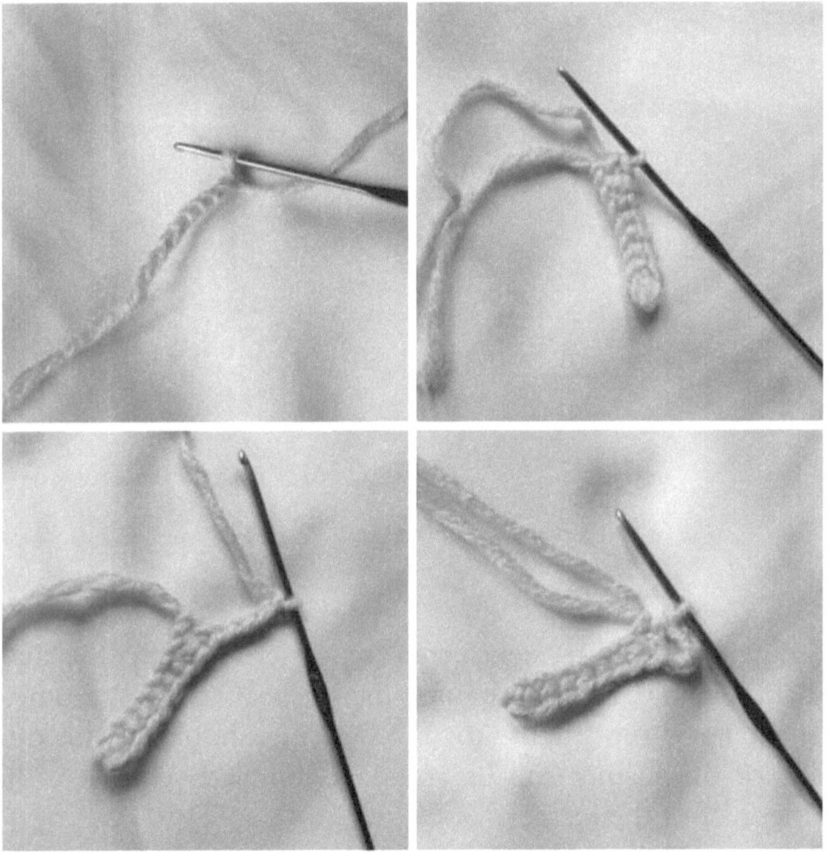

Feathers: Chain 8 -10 as you wish. Now for the next row work 1 sc into each chain. Chain 4 and slip stitch into the chain near hook. Again chain 4 and st into the next chain.

Ch5 and st into the next chain, repeat ch5, st into the next chain. Chain 6, st into the next chain, repeat *ch5, st* 2 times. Chain 4 and slip stitch into the chain next hook. By this one side of the feather will be complete. Similarly complete the other half of the feather.

Use different coloured yarn to create 5-6 feathers.

Attach strings with the feather on any one side and then attach

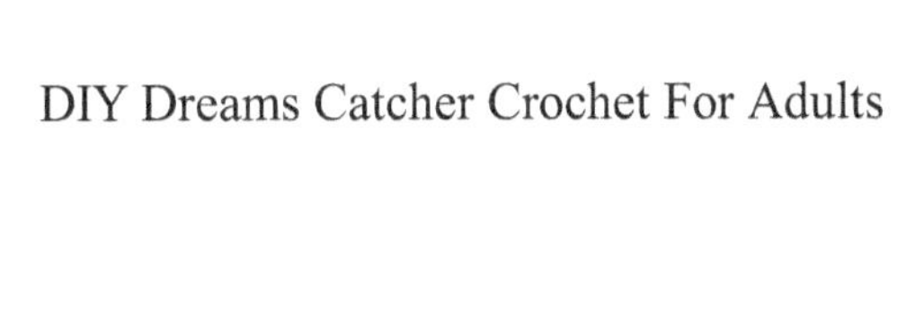

the feathers on any one side of the doily frame using the strings.

Attach a hanging mechanism to complete the dreamcatcher.

White Crochet Dreamcatcher

"Dreamcatchers were traditionally used by The First Nations of North America to protect children from nightmares. I loved the idea of celebrating historical traditions while coming up with something new to crochet.

I decided to add a vibrant set of colours to a Granny-style doily to create a simple, pretty design. Colourblocked felt feathers also add a touch of whimsy. The long adjustable string lets you easily untie and re-tie it wherever you want – hang it from a window, keep it in a nook in your hallway, or display it at your desk. And because it's so quick and easy, you'll probably find yourself wanting to whip up more dreamcatchers – luckily your local craft shop should have all the supplies."

Follow the crochet dreamcatcher pattern below to make your own, then share your makes using #molliemakers.

You will need:

• The supplies in your free kit from Mollie Makes 54

• 15m 100% cotton yarn in white

• 3mm (UK10, US D/3) crochet hook

• 10cm (4") hoop

• Coloured felt

• Feather template from issue 54

• Yarn needle, for sewing ends

Measurements

The finished dreamcatcher is 10cm (4") diameter with a fringe approx. 12cm (4¾") long.

Tension

Tension is not important for this project, just aim for a finish you are happy with.

Abbreviations

Crochet abbreviations conversions

Use this handy table to convert UK crochet terms to US crochet terms, or vice versa.

UK		US	
chain	ch	chain	ch
slip stitch	ss	slip stitch	ss
double crochet	dc	single crochet	sc
half treble	htr	half double	hdc
treble	tr	double	dc
double treble	dtr	treble	tr
triple treble	ttr	double treble	dtr

Simply Crochet UK-to-US conversion chart

You Will Need

Crochet hook

Yarn

Felt

Total time:

An afternoon

Step 1

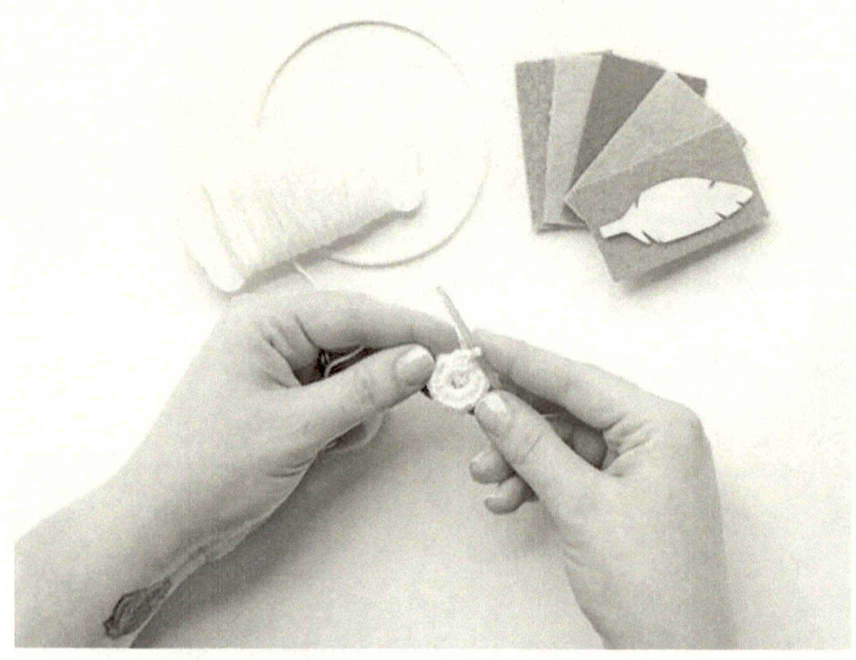

How to make a crochet dreamcatcher step 1

Round 1 ch8, ss to first ch to form a ring.

Step 2

How to make a crochet dreamcatcher step 2

Round 2 ch2 (counts as first dc in this round and all following), 15dc in ring, join into the top of the 2nd ch from start with a ss [16dc]

Step 3

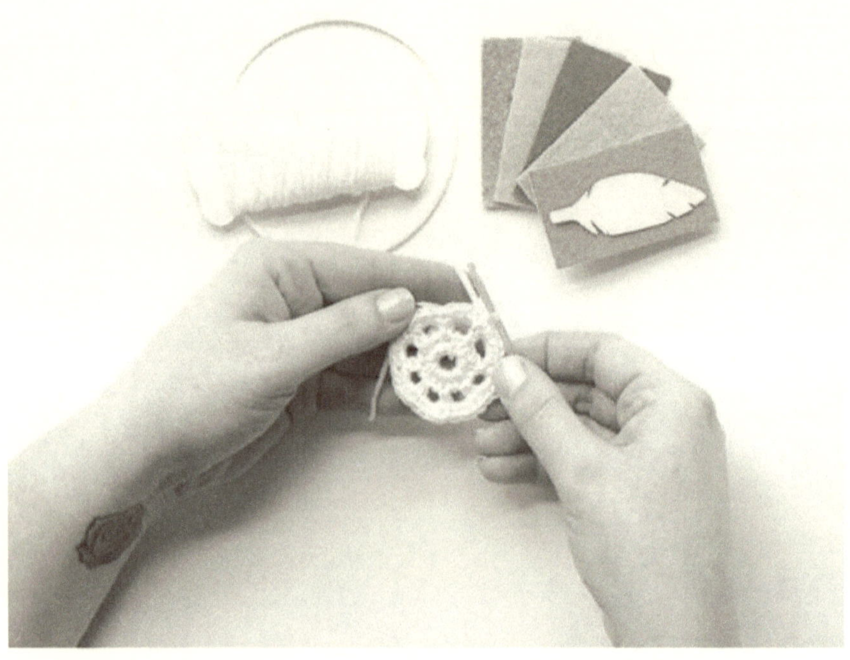

How to make a crochet dreamcatcher step 3

Round 3 ch2, ch3, *miss 1 st, 1dc in next st, ch3; repeat from * to end of round finishing with miss 1 st, join into the top of the 2nd ch from start with a ss [8 3ch-sps]

Step 4

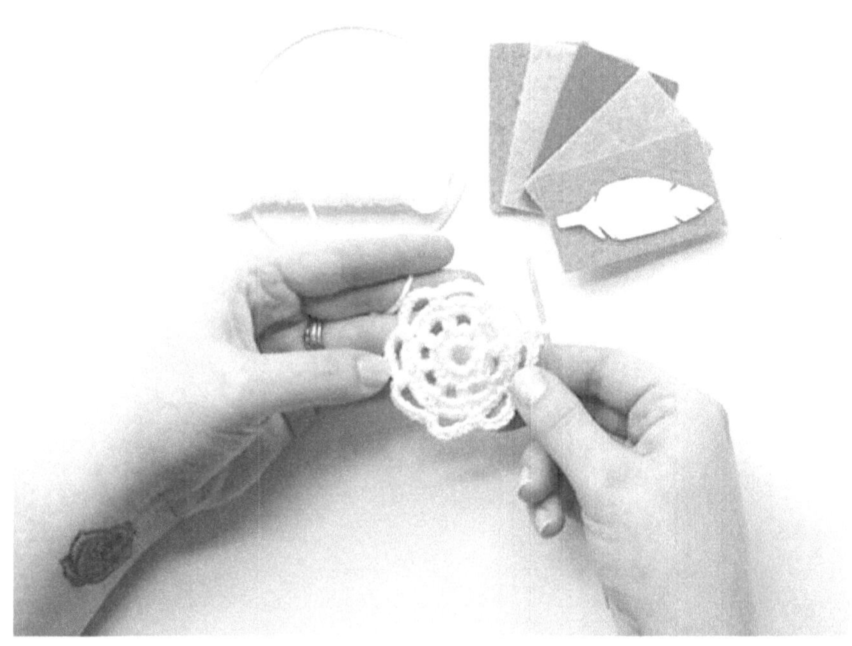

How to make a crochet dreamcatcher step 4

Round 4 ss into first 3ch-sp, ch2, 3dc in same 3ch-sp, 4dc in each of next 7 3ch-sps, join into the top of the 2nd ch from start with a ss [32dc]

Step 5

How to make a crochet dreamcatcher step 5

Round 5 ch2, ch6, *miss 3 sts, 1dc in next st, ch6; repeat from * to end of round; finishing with miss 3 sts, join into the top of the 2nd ch from start with a ss [8 6ch-sps]

Step 6

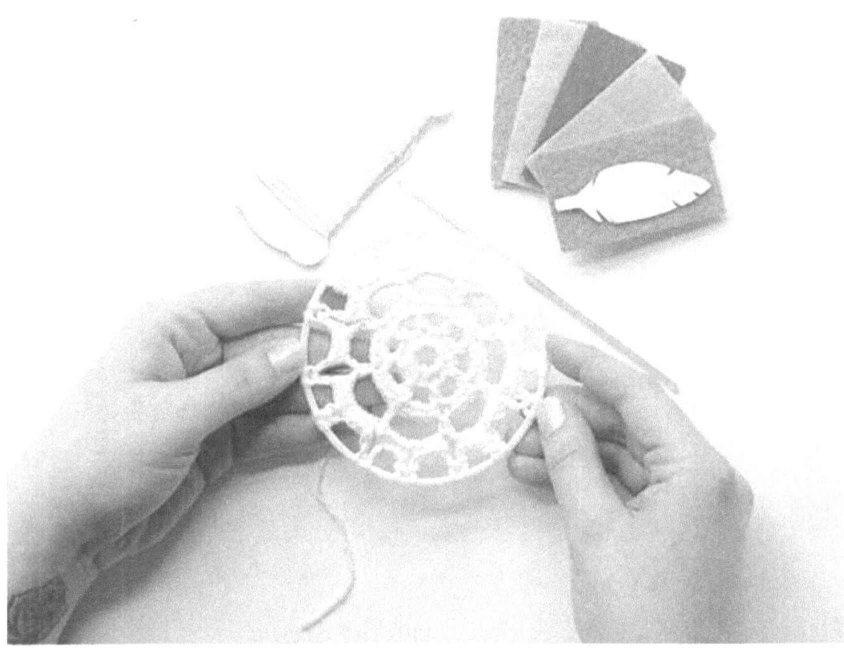

How to make a crochet dreamcatcher step 6

Round 6 ss into first 6ch-sp, ch2, 3dc in same 6ch-sp, ch2, ss around hoop (note: here and at all ss on this round, hold yarn at back of hoop so when you do the next ch st you bring the yarn over the top of the hoop again, giving it an extra secure join), ch2, 4dc in the same 6ch-sp, ch2, ss around 10 cm hoop, ch2, *(4dc, ch2, ss around 10 cm hoop, ch2, 4dc, ch2, ss around 10 cm hoop, ch2) all in next 6ch-sp; repeat from * to end of round; join into the top of the 2nd ch from start with a ss. Break yarn, fasten off and sew in ends.

Finishing

Step 1

How to make a crochet dreamcatcher step 7

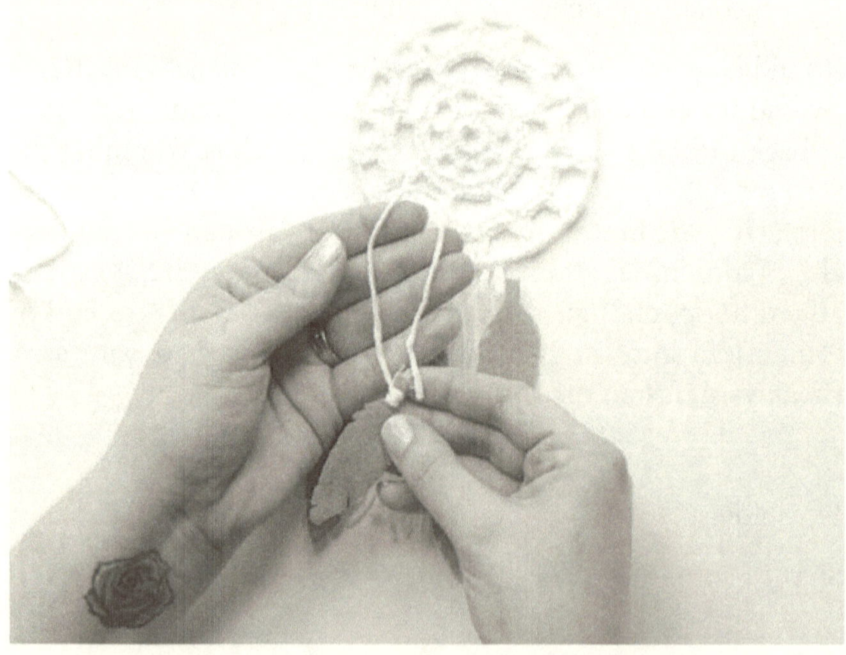

How to make a crochet dreamcatcher step 8

Cut 12 25cm (97/8") pieces of yarn and tie each one in half around the hoop to form the fringe. Using the feather template opposite, cut out five felt feathers and attach, with yarn, over the fringe. Make an 80cm (31½") chain as a tie and attach it to the top of the dreamcatcher for hanging.

Crochet dreamcatcher complete. Hang yours above your bed and scare all the bad dreams away!

Crochet Color Dream Catcher

Crochet Terms: US

Finished Size: 250mm once attached to the loop and including loop

Materials Used:

Yarn:

DMC Natura Just Cotton in the following colours. I crocheted each round in order of colour.

Col A – Amaranto

Col B – Spring Rose

Col C – Acanthe

Col D – Ble

Col E – Light Green

Col F – Jade

Col G – Aquamarine

Col H – Bleu Layette

Col I – Blue Jeans

Hook: Size 3.5mm was used but I would recommend a 3.25mm to have the crocheted piece stretch more when attached onto the ring.

Ring: 250mm ring (I used a Shamrock Craft Plastic Beige 250mm ring from Spotlight)

Yarn needle

Scissors

Ribbon or lace of your choice

Stitches and Abbreviations used:

Chain (ch)

Single Crochet (sc): Starting with a loop on your hook, insert hook in stitch or space indicated and draw up a loop (two loops on hook). Yarn over and pull through both loops on your hook.

Standing Single Crochet: Starting with a slip stitch on your hook, insert hook in stitch or space indicated and draw up a loop (two loops on hook). Yarn over and pull through both loops on your hook.

Half Double Crochet (hdc): Starting with a loop on your hook, yarn over, insert hook in stitch or space indicated, yarn over and draw up a loop (three loops on hook. Yarn over and pull through all three loops.

Double Crochet (dc): Starting with a loop on your hook, yarn over, insert hook in stitch or space indicated, yarn over and draw up a loop (three loops on hook). Yarn over and pull through two loops (two loops on hook). Yarn over and pull through both loops on your hook.

Standing Double Crochet: Starting with a slip stitch on your hook, yarn over, insert hook in stitch or space indicated, yarn over and draw up a loop (three loops on hook). Yarn over and pull through two loops (two loops on hook). Yarn over and pull through both loops on your hook.

Treble Crochet (tr): Starting with a loop on your hook, yarn over twice, insert hook in stitch or space indicated, yarn over and draw up a loop (4 loops on hook). (Yarn over and pull through two loops) x 3 times

Cluster 2 (cl2): Starting with a loop on your hook, *yarn over, insert hook in stitch or space indicated, yarn over and draw up a loop (3 loops on hook), yarn over and pull through two loops*, repeat from * once, yarn over and pull through all (4) loops.

Cluster 3 (cl3): Starting with a loop on your hook, *yarn over, insert hook in stitch or space indicated, yarn over and draw up a loop (3 loops on hook), yarn over and pull through two loops*, repeat from * two times, yarn over and pull through all loops.

Standing cl2: Starting with a slip stitch on your hook, *yarn over, insert hook in stitch or space indicated, yarn over and draw up a loop (3 loops on hook), yarn over and pull through two loops*, repeat from * twice, yarn over and pull through all loops.

V stitch (v st): dc, ch 3, dc in same sp

V treble stitch (v-tr): tr, ch 3, tr in same sp

Join with slip stitch (jss)

Pattern:

Round 1:

Using Col A; in a magic ring, ch 3 (counts as dc), 15 dc in ring, jss to top of ch 3 made.

(16 dc)

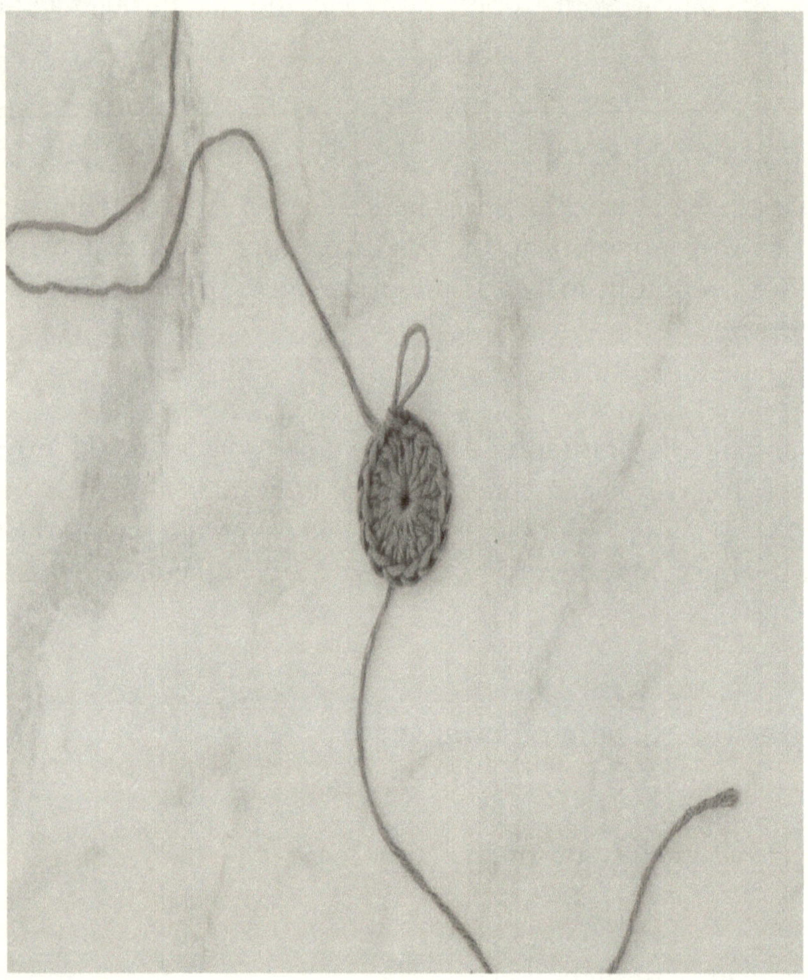

Round 2:

Using Col A; Ch 4 (counts as dc + ch), (dc + ch 1) in each st around, jss to 3rd ch made. Cut yarn and fasten off.

(16 dc, 16 x ch-1 sp)

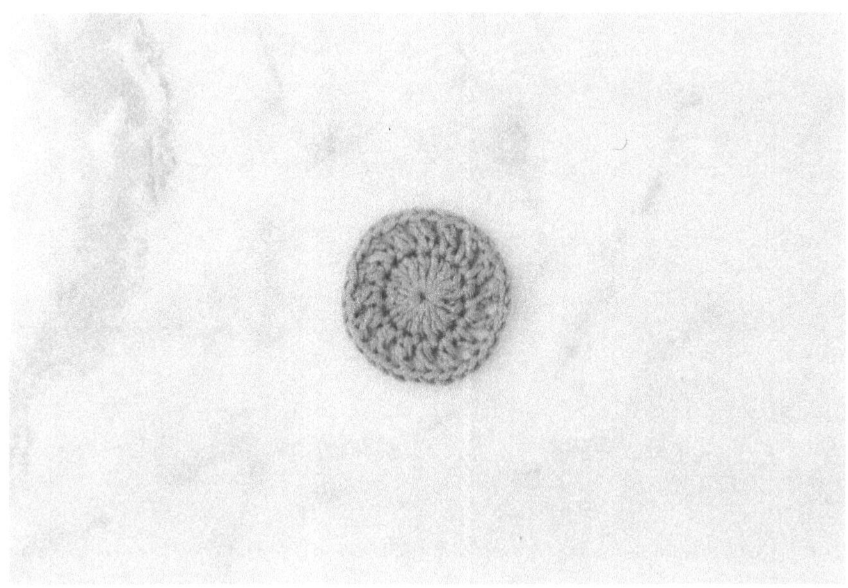

Round 3:

Using Col B; In any ch-1 sp, make a standing cl2, ch 5, (cl2, ch 5) in each ch-1 sp around, jss to 1st cl2 made. Cut yarn and fasten off.

(16 cl2, 16 x ch-5 sp)

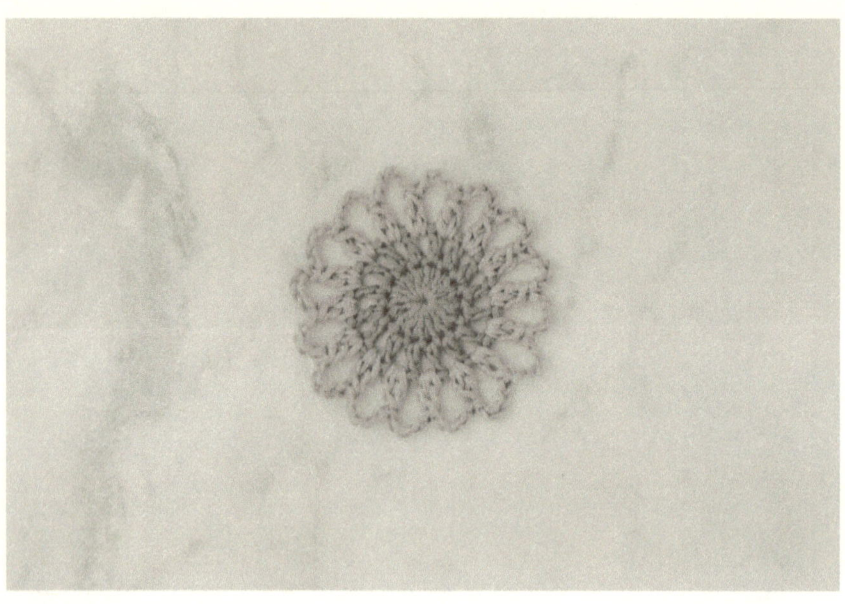

Round 4:

Using Col C; In any ch-5 sp, make a standing sc, ch 7, (sc, ch 7) in each ch-5 sp around, jss to 1st sc made. Cut yarn and fasten off.

(16 sc, 16 x ch-7 sp)

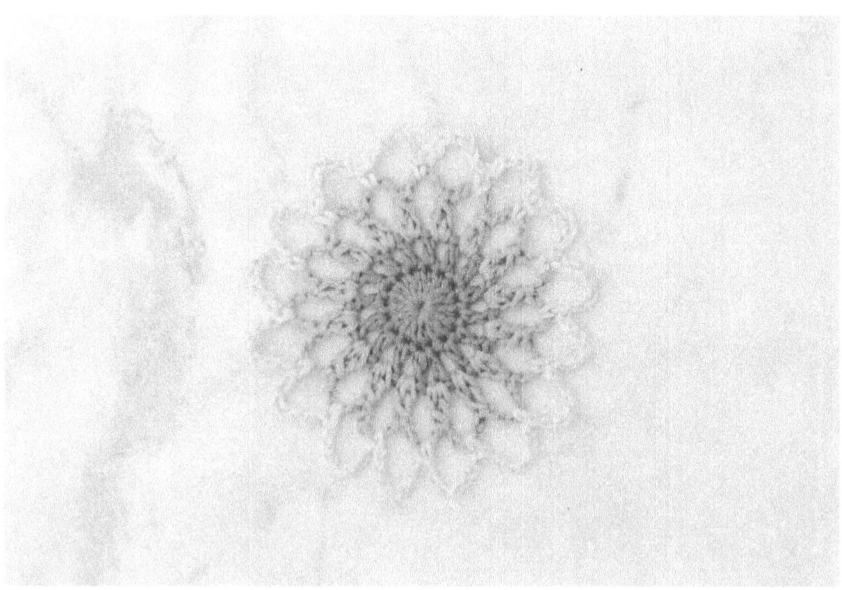

Round 5:

Using Col D; In any ch-7 sp, make a standing sc, ch 9, (sc, ch 9) in each ch-7 sp around, jss to 1st sc made. Cut yarn and fasten off.

(16 dc, 16 x ch-9 sp)

Round 6:

Using Col E; In any ch-9 sp, make a standing dc, 4 dc in same sp, ch 3, (5 dc, ch 3) in each ch-9 sp around, jss to 1st sc made. Cut yarn and fasten off.

(16 x 5 dc groups, 16 x ch-3 sp)

Round 7:

Using Col F; In any ch-3 sp, make a standing dc, (ch 3, dc) in same sp, ch 2, skip 2 dc, sc in next dc (middle dc of 5 dc group), ch 2, skip 2 dc, *v st in next ch-3 sp, ch 2, skip 2 dc, sc in next dc, ch 2, skip 2 dc*, repeat from * around, jss to 1st dc. Cut yarn and fasten off.

(16 x v st, 16 sc, 32 x ch-2 sp)

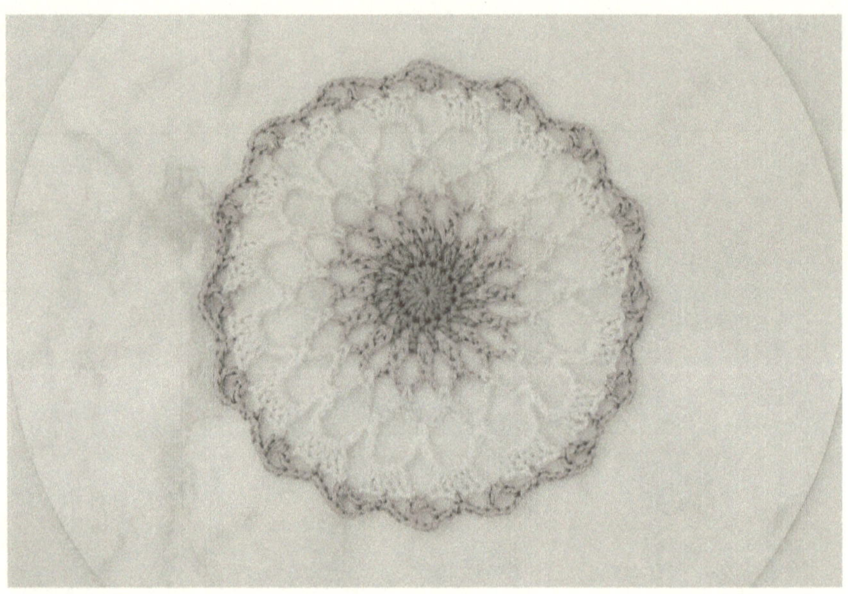

Round 8:

Using Col G; In any ch-3 sp from v st from round 7, make a standing cl3, ch 3, cl3 in same sp, ch 2, skip 2 ch sts, sc in sc from round 7, ch 2, skip 2 ch sts, *(cl3, ch 3, cl3) in next ch-3 sp, ch 2, skip 2 ch sts, sc in sc, ch 2, skip 2 ch sts*, repeat from * around, jss to top of 1st cl3 made. Cut yarn and fasten off.

(16 x [cl3, ch 3, cl3], 16 x sc, 32 x ch-2 sp)

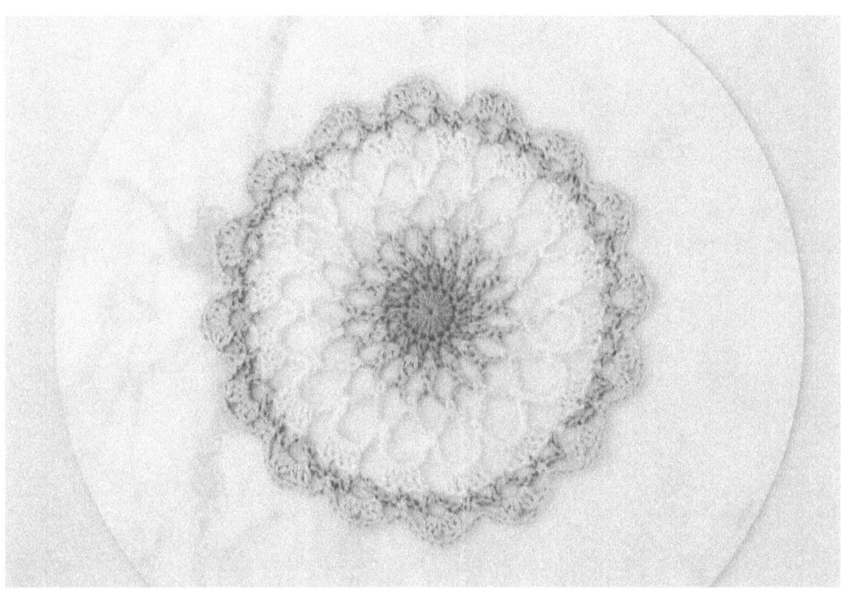

Round 9:

Using Col H; In any ch-3 sp made in round 8, make a standing dc, (ch 3, dc) in same sp, ch 1, skip 3 sts (cl3, 2 ch), v-tr in sc made in round 8, ch 1, skip 3 st (2 ch, cl3), *v st in ch-3 sp, ch 1, skip 3 sts, v-tr in sc, ch 1, skip 3 sts* repeat from * around, jss to 1st v st. Cut yarn and fasten off.

(16 x v st, 16 x v-tr, 16 x sc, 32 x ch-1 sp)

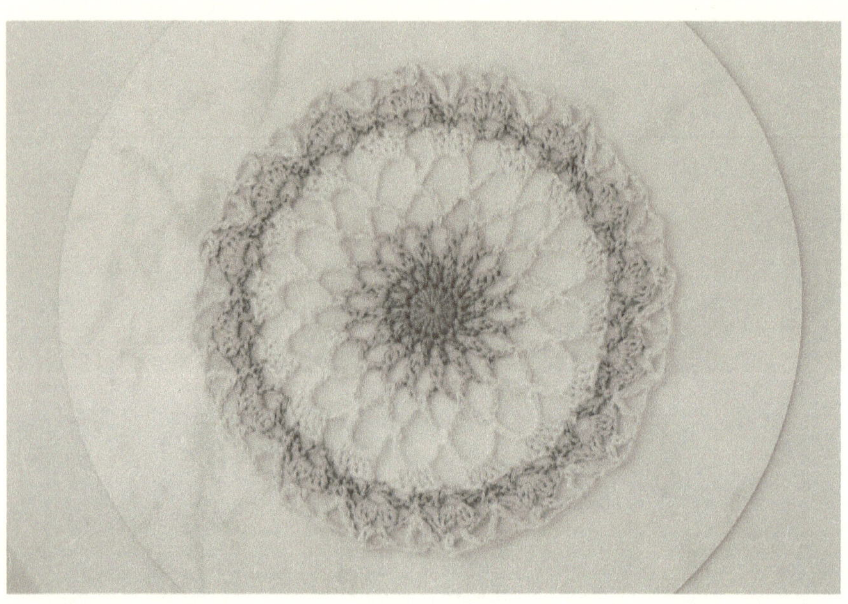

Round 10:

Using Col I; In any ch-3 sp (it doesn't matter if it's from the v st or v-tr st), make a standing sc, (sc, ch 1 2 sc) in same sp, skip st, sc in ch-1 sp, skip st, (2 sc, ch 1, 2 sc) in ch-3 sp, skip st, sc in ch-1 sp*, repeat from * around, jss to 1st sc made. Cut yarn and weave in ends.

(160 sc, 32 x ch-1)

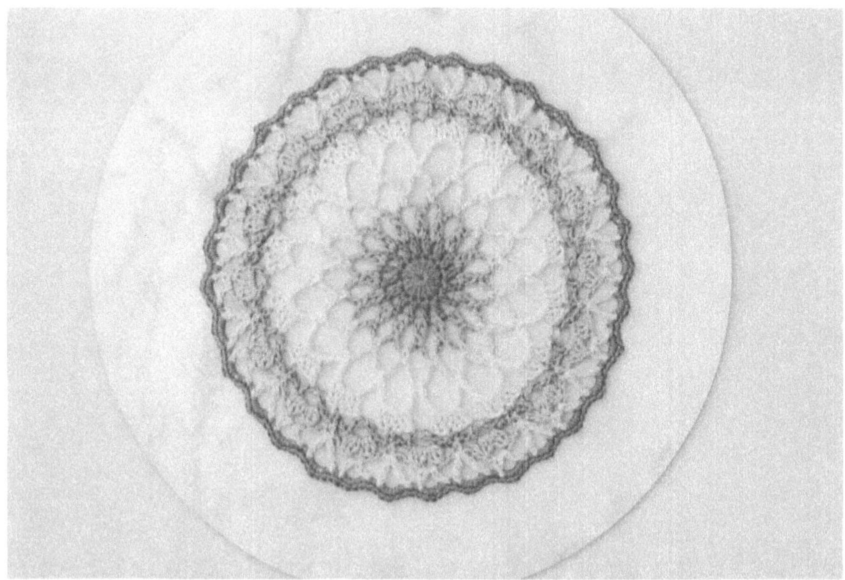

To attach to hoop, cut a piece of yarn the same material that you just used about 1m/40 inches. Thread onto needle, insert needle through ch-1 sp of any 'point' made in the last round, holding the crocheted part inside the hoop, thread needle under hoop, bringing it back over the top and into the next ch -1 sp, repeat around and fasten off, weave in yarn.

To get the same look as this new dream catcher, repeat this, but go the other way so you criss-cross over the ones already made.

Cut ribbon/lace into desired length and attach to bottom oh hoop using a slip knot method. I think it's called something like that, Fold ribbon in half and insert the middle (loop part) through the sp created when attaching crocheted part to hoop, pull wrap over the 'legs' of the ribbon, they just look like hanging legs to me lol, so that it creates a loop. Ta da ☺.

So there you have it! I just love how the colours look, rainbows are just beautiful 🌈. I hope you like the update and make some yourself. Please don't forget to add this pattern to your Ravelry Project….

Also if you have Instagram use the hashtag #loopydreamcatcher that way, I can see it there too.

ORIGINAL VERSION:

Howdy Doody! I thought I'd share a new pattern with you all. So here it is… (this photo is of the crocheted work facing the wrong way, I put the ribbon on back to front ☺)

Materials:

– I used Patons 4ply Cotton in Black

– 3.25mm recommended hook

– Scissors

– Yarn needle

– 10 inch / 25.5cm hoop (bought this one from Lincraft for the Aussies)

– Ribbon or lace for detail

Notes:

– This pattern is written in US terms

– Not as hard as you think ☺

Stitches and Abbreviations Used:

– sc = single crochet

– ch = chain

– ch sp = chain sp

– dc = double crochet

– dc2tog = double crochet 2 together

-dc3tog = double crochet 3 together

– tr = treble

-sl st = slip stich

Pattern:

1: Make magic ring, ch3, 15dc in ring, join with sl st (16sts)

2: ch4 counts as dc + ch1, (dc + ch1) in each st around join with sl st (16sts)

3: sl st to ch sp, (ch2 counts as start of dc2tog), dc in same sp, ch5, (dc2tog + ch5) in each ch sp around, join with sl st to first dc2tog (16 loops)

4: sl st in first 2 sts of ch5, sc into ch sp, ch7, *(sc in next sp + ch7)* repeat around, join with sl st to first sc (16 loops)

5: sl st in first 3 sts of ch7, sc into ch sp, ch 9, *(sc in next sp + ch9)* repeat around, join with sl st to first sc (16 loops)

6: sl st in first 4 sts of ch9, (ch 3, 3dc) in same sp, ch3, (5dc + ch3) in each sp around, make dc in the first loop (beginning ch-9 sp you worked in), (16x 5dcs)

7: sl st in next to sts so that you are in the middle dc from previous round, ch3 counts as sc + ch 2, *(dc, ch3, dc) in next sp, ch 2, sc in middle dc from previous round, ch 2* repeat around 14 more times, (dc, ch3, dc) in next sp, ch 2, join to first sc with sl st.

8: ch3 (counts as sc + ch2), *(dc3tog, ch2, dc3tog) in next ch3 sp, ch 2, sc into sc from previous round, ch2*, repeat around 14 more times, (dc3tog, ch 3, dc3tog) in next sp, ch2, join with sl st to 1st ch of ch3 at the beginning of the round.

9: ch7 (counts as tr + ch3), tr in same st, ch1, *(dc, ch3, dc) in sp between dc3togs from previous round, ch1, (tr, ch3, tr) into sc from previous round, ch1* repeat around 14 more times, (dc, ch3, dc) in next sp between dc3tog, ch1, join with sl st to the 4th ch.

10: *(2sc, ch2, 2sc) in ch3 sp, sc in next ch1 sp*, repeat around and join with sl st to first sc. Cut, secure yarn and weave in end.

To attach to hoop, cut a piece of yarn the same material that you just used about 1m/40 inches. Thread onto needle, insert needle through ch2 sp of any 'point' made in the last round, holding the crocheted part inside the hoop, thread needle under hoop, bringing it back over the top and into the next ch2 sp, repeat around and fasten off, weave in yarn.

Cut ribbon/lace into desired length and attach to bottom oh hoop using a slip knot method. I think it's called something like that, Fold ribbon in half and insert the middle (loop part) through the sp created when attaching crocheted part to hoop, pull wrap over the 'legs' of the ribbon, they just look like hanging legs to me lol, so that it creates a loop. Kind of like when you attach tassels to blankets, my brain has gone blank, I am not even sure if you call them tassels now lol. Sleep deprivation will do that to you.

I hope you enjoy making your own dream catcher – they are a lot easier than you think they would be. Emily ☺

DIY Big Dream Catcher

Have big dreams? Then, you need a big dreamcatcher, because sometimes just any old dream catcher won't do.

Ready to catch some big dreams??

HOW TO MAKE A BIG DREAMCATCHER

1. You'll need a large embroidery hoop.

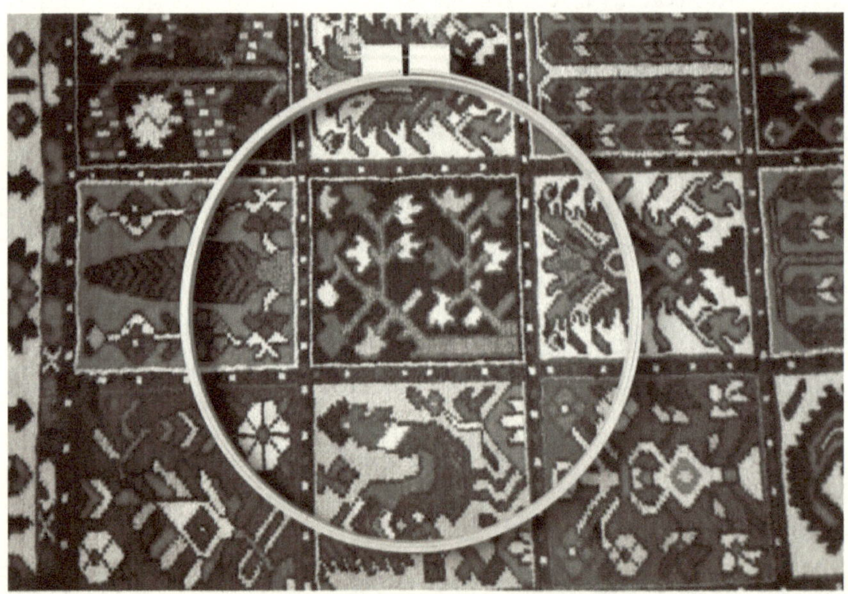

2. Take the hoop apart. We'll only need the inner hoop.

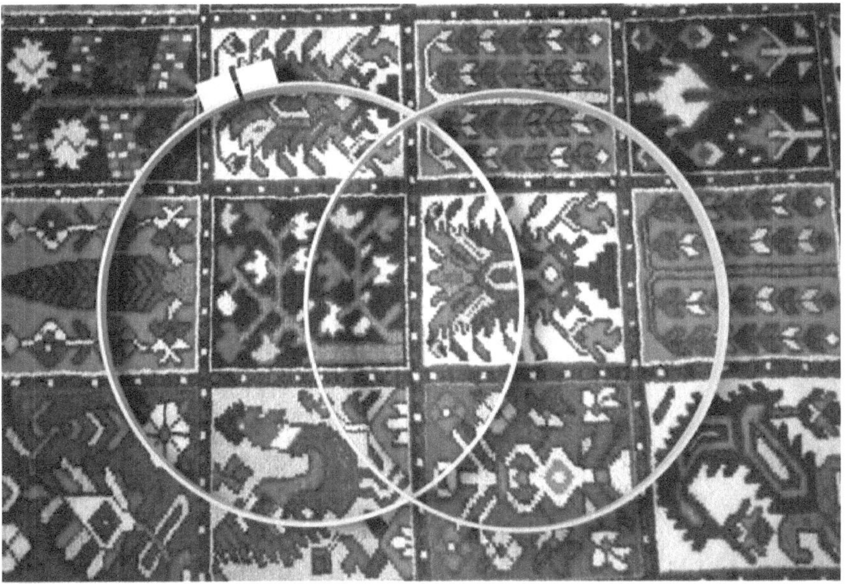

3. Wrap yarn around the hoop. I used a macrame technique shown in this video at Lune Vintage.

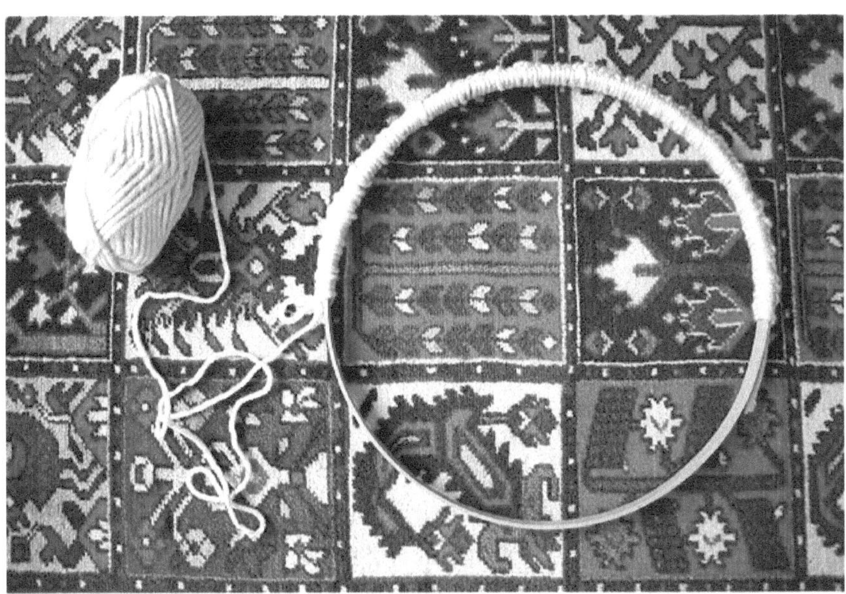

4. Next, you'll need a supersized doily. I crocheted my own by starting with this pattern and improvising towards the end when the gauge got wonky. UPDATE: The yarn I used was Lion Brand's Hometown USA in Houston Cream. Thanks for asking Monica!

If you don't crochet, don't worry. You can purchase doilies at thrift and antique stores and sew them together to fill in the area in the hoop. This is similar to how the the girls at A Beautiful Mess did here.

5. Next, tie the edges of the doily to the hoop with thread. Finally, add tassels and embellishments. I chose pearls, but there are a lot of other great ideas in this post.

Alright gals, dream on…. What are you dreaming of?

Pineapple Snowflake Suncatcher

Skill: Easy

Size: About 11" round

Materials: Size 10 Crochet Thread (Knit-Cro-Sheen): White – 75 yards; Brass Ring – 11" round; Large Sewing Needle; ¼" wide Satin Ribbon – Peach, 8" long; Ribbon Rose – Peach; Hot Glue.

Note: Since Cotton stretches over time it's a good idea to make sure your piece is a tight fit when sewing it onto the ring. You may want to increase the ring size for a tighter fit depending on the size of your piece.

Crochet Hook: Steel size 7 (1.65 mm) or size needed to obtain gauge.

Gauge: Rnd 1 = 1¾"

Special Stitches

Cluster Stitch (cl-st): Keeping last lp of each st on hook, work 3 tr or 5 tr in st or sp indicated, yo and draw through all lps on hook.

SUNCATCHER

Rnd 1: (Right Side) Starting at center, ch 6, join with sl st to first ch to form ring; ch 4, keeping last lp of ea st on hook work 4 tr in ring, yo, draw through all lps on hook (beg cluster made), ch 7, (5 tr cl-st in ring, ch 7) 5 times; join with sl st to top of beg cl-st. (6 cl-sts)

DO NOT TURN EACH ROUND.

Rnd 2: Ch 1, (sc, hdc, 7dc, hdc, sc) in next ch-7 sp around; join with sl st to first sc. (6 Shells)

Rnd 3: Ch 8 (counts as first dc and ch 5), dc in same st as

joining, ch 5, sc in center dc of next shell, * ch 5, (dc, ch 5, dc) in sp between next 2 shells, ch 5, sc in center dc of next shell; rep from * around; ending with ch 2, dc in first dc (this join brings thread in position for next Rnd). (12 dc, 6 sc)

Rnd 4: Ch 1, sc in same sp as joining, ch 3, (dc, ch 1) 7 times in next ch-5 sp, ch 2, sc in next ch-5 sp, * ch 5, sc in next ch-5 sp, ch 3, (dc, ch 1) 7 times in next ch-5 sp, ch 2, sc in next ch-5 sp; rep from * around, ending with ch 2, dc to first sc. (42 dc, 12 sc)

Rnd 5: Ch 1, sc in same sp as joining, ch 3, (3 tr cl-st in next ch-1 sp, ch 1) 3 times, ch 2, (3 tr cl-st in next ch-1 sp, ch 1) 3 times, ch 2, * sc in next ch-5 sp, ch 3, (3 tr cl-st in next ch-1 sp, ch 1) 3 times, ch 2, (3 tr cl-st in next ch-1 sp, ch 1) 3 times, ch 2, rep from * around, join with sl st to first sc. (36 Clusters)

Rnd 6: Ch 9 (counts as first tr and ch 5), ** (3 tr cl-st in next ch-1 sp, ch 2) twice, (3 tr cl-st, ch 5, 3 tr cl-st) in ch-3 sp, (ch 2, 3 tr cl-st in next ch-1 sp) twice,** ch 5, * tr in next sc, ch 5, (3 tr cl-st in next ch-1 sp, ch 2) twice, (3 tr cl-st, ch 5, 3 tr cl-st) in ch-3 sp, (ch 2, 3 tr cl-st in ch-1 sp) twice, ch 5, rep from * around, join with sl st to first tr. (36 Clusters)

Rnd 7: Ch 9 (counts as first tr and ch 5), tr in same ch as joining, ch 3, (3 tr cl-st in next ch-1 sp, ch 2) twice, (3 tr cl-st, ch 5, 3 tr cl-st) in ch-3 sp, (ch 2, 3 tr cl-st in next ch-1 sp) twice, ch 3, * (tr, ch 5, tr) in next tr, ch 3, (3 tr cl-st in next ch-1 sp, ch 2) twice, (3 tr cl-st, ch 5, 3 tr cl-st) in ch-3 sp, (ch 2, 3 tr cl-st in next ch-1 sp) twice, ch 3, rep from * around, join with sl st to first tr. Finish off and weave in ends.

Finishing

– Using Needle and Crochet Thread, stretch and sew points to Brass ring.

– Tie a 2½" Bow and glue to center of Suncatcher.

– Glue Rose over center of Bow.

www.ingramcontent.com/pod-product-compliance
Lightning Source LLC
Chambersburg PA
CBHW021357160726
47994CB00007B/2995